CUTtiNgS
2
The pick of COUNTRY LIFE from Punch

D0873622

CUTTINGS 2

The pick of COUNTRY LIFE from Punch

Compiled by Carole Mansur

Cartoons by Geoffrey Dickinson

Elm Tree Books/London

First published in Great Britain 1981
by Elm Tree Books/Hamish Hamilton Ltd
Garden House 57–59 Long Acre London WC2E 9JZ

Copyright © 1981 by Punch Publications Ltd
Cartoons copyright © 1981 by Geoffrey Dickinson

Book design by Glyn Rees

British Library Cataloguing in Publication Data
Cuttings.
   2.
   1. English wit and humor
   2. Country life—Great Britain—
   Anecdotes, facetiae, satire, etc.
   I. Mansur, Carole   II. Dickinson, Geoffrey
   III. Punch
   827'.91408'03241   PN6231.C65
   ISBN 0–241–10656–7

Printed and bound in Great Britain by
Richard Clay (The Chaucer Press) Ltd, Bungay, Suffolk

Foreword

One of the most popular items in PUNCH is not—to the annoyance of the PUNCH writers—produced by the PUNCH writers at all. The 'Country Life' column, consisting of cuttings snipped from such publications as the *Ilkley Gazette* and the *Slough Observer*, is produced by reporters and sub-editors who have no idea that their words will ever get further than the next edition of their papers. They do, thanks to the alertness of readers who send them into PUNCH.

What makes a 'Country Life' snippet? It is hard to describe but we know it when we see it. Sometimes it is a misprint, sometimes an unfortunate juxtaposition. Or it is a story, hitherto confined to a local paper, which seems worthy of wider exposure, like the *Western Gazette*'s scoop of the monk and the runner beans and the *Hawick Express*'s exposure of the Brillo Pad in Nuclear Shelter Scandal. Then there was the South Pole shopping spree that shook Antarctica, the Banbury Parachutists, the defendant accused of being in possession of five O-levels, the . . . but the pages that follow will give the general idea.

The popularity of the column has been proved by the success of the first anthology, CUTTINGS, published last year. Here is the second volume, dedicated this time, not to the sub-editors, who failed to spot the mirth-making potential of the words that passed in front of them, but to the readers who did.

A former tax officer was fined by local magistrates for stealing a bread roll and a packet of ham and a pair of running shoes from a High Street store. He took the shoes because he needed to get around the kitchen.

M. Miller *(Bournemouth Evening Echo)*

She told the police and they found Fletton the same evening hiding in the men's toilets in Cambridge Street. He was wearing nothing but a ladies black half slip. When questioned he admitted having been in the ladies' toilet, but he said he did not mean any harm, he was just being sociable.

G. Ridgewell *(Tring Advertiser and Aylesbury News)*

A barrister, Mr David Bentley, declared: "Adultery may be rather fashionable in some places, but we are not talking about Knightsbridge or Chelsea. We are talking about Barnsley, and in Barnsley, where we call a spade a shovel, trying to knock somebody else's wife off is not well thought of."

M. Robinson *(Yorkshire Post)*

"The Isle of Wight is an island, surrounded by water, as indeed are all islands," he said in his opening remarks.

M. Lewis *(Big Farm Weekly)*

The case had originally been heard at the end of August, but because a juror tried to tell a witness a joke about an octopus the judge ordered a retrial.

M. Morgan *(South London Press)*

Already provisionally booked for next year's Ludlow Festival is Alec Clifton-Taylor, the man who appeared in the popular television series, "Six English Towns". It is thought he will give a talk on small Georgian houses, some of which will probably be in Ludlow.

D. Arney *(Ludlow Advertiser)*

A deaf-and-dumb parachutist faced a communications problem when he ended up suspended 30 ft. above the ground in a tree at Wheldrake, near York.

P. Hollindale *(Yorkshire Evening Press)*

He said closure would also cause problems for travellers, as the toilets were the last ones before Whalley for people travelling out of town and the first ones before the town centre for people coming in.

U. Hindle *(Blackburn Citizen)*

Rivers in the Pittsburgh district were generally stationary this morning and will continue to be so.

B. Pimm-Smith *(Pittsburgh Post-Gazette)*

Christmas is only three weeks away and plans are now well in hand for the festivities at the various centres. All centres will be closed on Christmas Day, Boxing Day and New Year's Day.

I. Heath *(British Airways News)*

Since taking on the British Leyland franchise four months ago business in the service and repair section has shot up 100 per cent.

P. James *(Birmingham Evening Mail)*

Tempers rose at Woking's dole queue on Monday morning when the annual influx of students and school-leavers swelled the queue and delayed the weekly handout by about an hour. "It's ridiculous," said one man impatiently, while a woman who tried to push to the top of the queue fulminated: "If this continues, I'll have to think seriously about finding a job."

M. Clarke *(Woking News and Mail)*

After he was turned out of a Kidderminster woman's home, Michael Trevor Dewick went back and stole her lawn mower. "I took it for sentimental reasons," he told police. "We had both used it and I intended to keep it as a memento."

M. Carter *(Kidderminster Times)*

A man seen in a telephone box with a hammer, chisel and pincers told police that he was taking his dog for a walk.

R. Kilby *(Coventry Evening Telegraph)*

A 26-year-old woman jumped from a bridge in Richmond, Virginia, in a suicide bid but climbed out complaining the water was too cold.

K. Hobbs *(Lancs Evening Post)*

Coun Hugh Walpole warned that if he had to pay ten pence to park for a couple of minutes in Louth town centre he might not buy his pork pies there in future.

J. Hill *(Louth Standard)*

He had been accused of falling asleep, so putting the ship, its passengers and crew in danger. He was found guilty on an amended charge of dozing instead of falling asleep and was fined £40.

T. Pendle *(Stornaway Gazette)*

A new St Ives society has been formed to promote goodwill and friendship—but more than half the townsfolk are barred from joining.

F. Richards *(Cambridge Evening News)*

The free condoms, in seven colours of the rainbow, plus black, will be available, according to Mr Meechai, in two sizes, "Thai and European." An exhibition of condoms of all kinds, shapes and sizes will be displayed.

E. Farmer *(Bangkok Post)*

With the holiday in London on Monday there was a fairly quiet start to the week which lasted until it ended.

T. Wright *(Rand Daily Mail)*

In his evidence, Dr A. Visram, a medical practitioner at Kitale District Hospital, said that Otuane died after shock when his head was chopped off.

R. Bowker *(Sunday Standard, Nairobi)*

"They went purely and simply for what is a fairly simply for what is a fairly small quantity of the hard more," the senior partner said. He believes the thief knew what he had been after.

D. A. Winfield *(Oxford Mail)*

He stated that it was becoming surgical practice where a limb was severed cleanly to attempt to re-attach it, and in this case the boy's parents had the good sense to bring it with them.

M. Warburton *(The Anglo-Celt)*

President Moi hit out yesterday at alcoholics and heavy drinkers. "Excessive drinking is dangerous," he said, as he laid the foundation stone of the multi-million shilling Kenya Breweries' plant at Kisumu.

J. Walden *(Kenya Daily Nation)*

A 20ft Christ-like effigy made from fibre glass imitation loaves of bread which has been erected on the Arndale Centre wall at Middleton is not to be removed, although it offends a number of people. The figure, which faces a busy by-pass is made up of different types of loaves for the head, body and limbs, with the loins covered by an imitation Sunblest bread wrapper.

G. Porter *(Manchester Evening News)*

Colt 38 Special. Police Positive. Both 2″ and 4″ barrels are available. FREE box of ammunition with each gun sold with a copy of this ad. THE PERFECT CHRISTMAS PRESENT.

K. Walton *(South African Roodepoort Record)*

Wanted to purchase—violin, also, small bore shot gun in case.

I. Dixon *(Scottish Field)*

It must be rather difficult for a child to know what we mean when we tell him Jesus was the "Limb of God", when he has never seen a lamb.

M. Miller (*Sarnia Gazette*)

The first prize, two Cross Channel tickets to Le Havre, was won by Mr Barlow, of Winchester Prison.

V. Jones (*Hampshire Chronicle*)

As Lord Brand started to sentence McGhee he ordered him to stand up. McGhee, who is under four feet tall, informed the Judge that he was already standing.

A. McConnell (*Glasgow Herald*)

Professor Nancy Hirshberg of the University of Illinois, Chicago has completed a ten year study of what kind of men are attracted to which physical features. Men who like women with big breasts tend to be out-going, show-offy, independent and don't care to help other people. Women with big buttocks are guilty, self-abasing, introverted and socially inactive. Leggy women are preferred by men who are socially active, while the women are concerned with making a good impression. "What does all this mean?" "I don't know," Professor Hirshberg said.

R. Pooley (*The West Australian*)

"The kidnappers really panicked. They untied us and told us to say we were at a business meeting, even though it was about midnight. The police came in and we played our part—although I kept dropping hints like 'we're a little tied up at the moment'. Eventually the police asked for our names. 'Gravestock-Barnes' I said. The officer queried it so I asked him to let me write it down. I wrote 'help'. The officer took the piece of paper to the inspector who then came out with 'which one is Mr Help?' I almost died."

R. Conyers (*Thame and Risborough Times*)

The Government has concessions up its sleeve to ease the unemployment in the North-East. That's the bad news today as one of the Prime Minister's top employment men began a two-day visit of the region.

R. Wilson (*Newcastle Evening Chronicle*)

Good home wanted for pedigree nine-month-old red settee, innoculated, house-trained, good with children.

M. Woods (*Grimsby Evening Telegraph*)

He told Mr Justice Cusack that the beer crate was unusual. The motel usually used Schweppes or Babycham boxes to prop up the beds after having trouble with plastic bed legs.

J. Cochrane *(Yorkshire Post)*

They have been told by the council that they can surrender the ticket and get all their money back—but refunds are impossible.

J. Boyden *(Horley Advertiser)*

Pamler, of Larchfield Street, Darlington, said that at the station police searched nine of the 10 pairs of trousers he was wearing but found nothing.

C. Waine *(Lancashire Evening Post)*

Hooper had the "astonishing record" of five O-levels, three A-levels, a diploma in business studies and 19 previous convictions. He also had considerable musical ability.

D. Kirk *(Somerset County Gazette)*

A clinic promoting natural cures for illness is to open in Maidstone. It will be run by self-confessed clairvoyant Anne Owen and Ken Alexander, a psychotherapist and cromotherapist, from Tunbridge Wells. Mr Alexander, recently back from America, was not available for comment. Mrs Owen said he was in bed with flu.

M. Taylor *(Kent Messenger)*

During that time he studied pantomime at Leeds College of Building to gain further qualifications.

J. Smurthwaite *(Yorkshire Evening Post)*

Mr Conroy said he accepted the fact that people have the right to remain silent when speaking to the Press.

W. Conkey *(Glasgow Evening Times)*

Mr Douglas Cooke, a senior environmental health officer with Crewe and Nantwich Council, said the matter was one mass of bacteria, but, he added, apart from it the chops were good.

J. Greenaway *(Manchester Evening News)*

When the international jet-set chat about the fun spots of the western world, it is fair to assume that Newport does not crop up in their conversation very often.

K. Watkins *(South Wales Argus)*

Sword gang shoot up a cafe.

R. Ford *(Western Daily Press)*

Vandals are winning their battle to make Luton a worse place to live in.

T. Hopkins (*Luton Evening News*)

Police are warning shopkeepers in the Isle of Wight to be on the lookout for novelty pound notes that could be circulating in the area. The notes—thought to come from Denmark—have a nude woman in place of the Queen's head, but otherwise look genuine at a glance.

S. Longley (*Southern Evening Echo*)

A man who stole a ballcock from an Abergavenny public toilet did so "because the Almighty had told him it was to be done," the town's magistrates heard. But when asked what he was going to do with it, he said he did not know because God had not told him.

M. Powell (*Abergavenny Chronicle*)

Police, two fire appliances and an ambulance went to Colton Street at 3 o'clock this morning when a woman climbed to the end of a 100-foot jib on a 100-foot crane. When the woman was brought down half an hour later she told the police: "I only wanted to have a scream up there on my own."

C. Merrill (*Leicester Mercury*)

The Desert Song is the ideal family show—sex, intrigue and violence all dressed up with some very hummable tunes.

I. Brazier (*Skipton Evening Post*)

With the words "Congratulations to my darling wife for our first child. All my love, Russell," painted on his bald head, Howard acted as a human telegram to visit Elaine in the maternity wing at the hospital.

J. Taylor (*Staffordshire Evening Sentinel*)

Before he was sentenced Taylor said: "I wasn't aware you couldn't get drunk in a public place. I thought this was a free country. It seems that Welwyn Garden City after dark turns into a police state."

G. Ridgewell (*Watford Evening Echo*)

A motorist being questioned about the tax disc ate it to prevent a police inspector from seeing it.

R. Henderson (*Bradford Telegraph and Argus*)

For the record, police say there are more than 1,370 people called Brown in the Brighton area telephone book. "Of course that is not including those who are not on the telephone," said the spokesman.

S. Hector (*Brighton Evening Argus*)

He escorted ten of the world's prettiest girls on a guided tour of the Palace of Westminster. Then he winded and dined the contestants before getting back to Commons business.

G. Ridgewell *(Luton Evening Post)*

The ladies of the Helping Hand Society enjoyed a swap social evening. Everybody brought something they didn't need. Many of the ladies brought their husbands.

R. Bladen *(Manchester Evening News)*

"The school is next to a grave yard, so what is wrong with building a funeral parlour?" Thus said Councillor Edwards. "Let's breathe a bit of life into the place."

E. Ashe *(Hoylake and West Kirby News)*

The double decker's roof escaped damage as the bus was driven along a route where trees have been trimmed to avoid hitting double decker roofs.

J. Webb *(Exeter Express and Echo)*

Mrs Dorling gave her report on the annual meeting in London. She said that since first attending as a delegate ten years ago the number of hats had lessened.

E. Tapp *(Yarmouth Mercury)*

WANTED. Have you an animal in the shape of a teapot, eg. cat.

J. Sechiari *(Isle of Wight County Press)*

The sorry story of Craft Patterns Ltd., Redhill is almost over. The firm, which has kept some customers waiting over a year for expensive clock movements, was compulsorily wound up on March 3.

N. Braidwood *(Sunday Post)*

These refer to four separate stages in the consummation of a marriage. (No marriage is valid in canon law until it is consummated.) If any one of *erectio, introductio, penetratio* or *ejaculatio* is absent—or if they happen in the wrong order—the marriage is not properly consummated and thus not valid.

T. Ryan *(Irish Sunday Press)*

World boxing champion Alan Minter has been invited to lead a sponsored walk on Sunday, September 7, to raise money for the Ashdown Forest Appeal. The Forest Conservators want 2,500 people to join the West Hoathly fighter and other personalities on the trek through the forest. The money will go towards maintaining the forest as a place of natural peace and beauty.

N. Sherry *(East Grinstead Courier)*

She did not have visions of seeing Father Christmas coming ashore at the Helford Passage—but she did think she saw a boat landing illegal immigrants! Police checks in the area, however, proved it was probably the coast-guard vessel Aquamanda coming ashore with skin divers.

C. Keen *(The Helston Packet)*

A big police search was launched last night after a motorist was hijacked by a man brandishing a dinner fork.

T. Hopkins *(Luton Evening Post)*

The jury had also heard from Teena Childs of her horror when she read in newspaper reports that her husband had murdered six people. She said he was a "normal bloke", though he occasionally pulled out his toenails.

A. Jolley *(Ilford Redbridge Post and Pictorial)*

Applications received from November 11 to November 17, 1977: 4/1/3278U. Salamis Restaurant, St Aubin's Road, St Helier—change of use from shop selling tropical fish to take-away fish and chip/kebab etc.

M. Fearnley *(Jersey Evening Post)*

Radio Hallam is all set for the Remembrance Day ceremony tomorrow. Staff at the station recorded the two-minute silence yesterday.

K. Smith *(Sheffield Morning Telegraph)*

"Bognor is a remarkable place," said Mr Cartland. The town was visited by so many different people in the past, and some of the anecdotes connected with them are worth recording. He has already discovered that the author and poet G. K. Chesterton came to Bognor in 1906 and nearly had his hat blown off.

L. Smith *(Bognor Regis Observer)*

Mr Swendell, who is in his 60s, was said to have taken a little time getting out of bed due to a disability. He tried to telephone the police, but Makepeace pulled the connection out of the wall, said Sgt Preston. Makepeace told the court he was "deeply sorry" for what he had done, and had subsequently tried to ring Mr and Mrs Swendell to apologise but could not get through.

S. De Silva *(Herts Advertiser)*

Have you ever wondered about the incidence of broken marriages among biscuit technologists?

C. Waine *(Oldham Evening Chronicle)*

Andover Trades Council have warned the superpowers to lay down their nuclear arms—or face the consequences.

C. Heathcote *(Andover Advertiser)*

Open-plan stairs to be used by the Queen when she visits a new leisure complex are to be changed in case women fear they will show too much leg.

D. Ritchie *(Dundee Courier and Advertiser)*

Scout Tom Dexter from Flintham, near Newark, Notts, has won an award for sleeping in uncomfortable places for 14 nights. They included a toilet, a coal scuttle and a car boot.

R. Goddard *(Kent Evening Post)*

In 1977 and 1978, the Dominican Republic was swept by African Swine Fever. African Swine Fever cannot be contracted by journalists.

J. Wyldbore *(Caribbean Insight)*

According to one councillor ycsterday "the Parthenon in Greece and the Colosseum in Rome would have been demolished long ago if Glasgow District Council had been responsible for them."

T. McCormick *(Glasgow Herald)*

A divorcee, Mrs Barbara Tinti, was ordered yesterday to pay 35p compensation for a salami sausage she stole from a supermarket. In a statement she said: "It was an Italian-named sausage and I get sentimental over Italian things."

M. Robinson *(Yorkshire Post)*

Retired clergyman who feels cold in East Anglia will be grateful to hear of someone who will kindly knit two string vests for a fee of £5; sample submitted.

E. King *(Church Times)*

In the police station he rolled a cigarette in a £1 note and smoked it. When police officers remonstrated with him, he said he preferred £5 notes.

O. McIntosh *(The Scotsman)*

For parking in Beaufort Square no waiting area, Chepstow, Reginald William George Hollingshead, of the Rose and Crown, Tintern, was fined £10. He was also fined £5 for causing litter by "throwing into the open air" a penalty parking ticket.

N. Whitcombe *(Chepstow Weekly Argus)*

The highlight of today's proceedings came when the court played a tape recording of a speech Jiang made to the Peking Opera Troupe in September 1968. "I tell you, Liu Shaoqi is a big counterrevolutionary a renegade and a trahtnr, && Jh'nf b'n bd hd'rd tn r'x nn thd rbr'tbhx f'ddd rdbnrding. He deserves to be sentenced to death, to die by a thousand cuts." Jiang's sole response to the recording, portions of which were broadcast on Chinese television, was to acknowledge that the voice was hers. But she added, "I can't make out the contents of what I am saying."

J. Nicoll *(Washington Star)*

One-legged actor (under 25) with Devon accent and parrot, required for amateur production.

D. Turner *(Brighton Evening Argus)*

DISCO. Free admission until 9.30, after 9.30 £1.00. Girls free all night.

R. Hawes *(Eastern Evening News)*

Regional officials decided to remove the Brillo pads and toilet paper from the atomic shelter at St Boswell's HQ. With worldwide unease growing over the nuclear question, the Region decided to press into service the nerve centre of the Council's nuclear quarters after it had masqueraded as a cleaner's store for several years.

P. Aitken *(Hawick Express)*

Khalaf, who was receiving guests in an ornate salon yesterday, said that Hussein had been very generous to him during his stay in Jordan and divulged that the king would be providing him and Shak'a with ears, especially adapted for their handicaps.

D. Benjamin *(Jerusalem Post)*

Dawn is strictly a 20th-century lady, fiercely independent, madly practical—and totally aware of everything around her. Censorship, pollution, over-population, politics and the demise of the white rhino—all inextricably woven into her being.

A. van der Spuy *(South African Sunday Times)*

MONDAYS from 29th September (7.15—9.15 pm). WOODWORK. If there is sufficient demand, this course will run as a Metalwork class.

E. Ashe *(Evening Class Syllabus)*

Unbreakable tea set, six plates, six saucers, five cups, £4.

J. Webster *(Enfield Advertiser)*

More than a 100 holiday makers flew out of Dublin last night to see the Pope in Rome. The Pilgrims booked seats months before it was known that the Pope was to visit Ireland. Most of them decided to go ahead with the trip.

W. Maclean *(Glasgow Herald)*

Well over half of the men and women over 85 cannot cut their own toenails, according to a survey published by the Government.

M. Joyce *(Lancashire Evening Telegraph)*

A new organisation composed mainly of people who don't have telephones has announced plans to field its own candidates for the Knesset. The new "Telephone Consumers Organisation", led by Tirazi Rom, called for a phone-in tomorrow, with the public calling the telephone service to explain the problems of not having a telephone.

K. Weinberger *(Jerusalem Post)*

"I told our guard commander, Corporal Tapera, that there were people advancing who were armed," he said. "I did not believe they were going to fire at us." Corporal Tapera came out of the room, saw the men advancing and returned to get his beret, said Rifleman Parewa.

J. Bullett *(Salisbury Herald)*

A Birmingham Councillor is being flown home from Hong Kong at a cost to ratepayers of nearly £1,000, so he can attend tomorrow's City Council meeting to discuss public spending cuts.

J. Brockington *(Birmingham Evening Mail)*

"She added she did not want them taken away because she loved animals. In connection with the under feeding of the Dane, she said both she and Bell thought it did not need all that much food as she thought it was a whippet."

T. Emmott *(Ormskirk Advertiser)*

Speaker at the Pyrford Women's Institute meeting was Mrs Beech—who was mentioned in Hansard when, as a wife of an MP, she was rebuked by the Speaker of the House of Commons for rustling a newspaper during a debate.

D. Lawton *(Woking News and Mail)*

These are the big big bales produced by one of the earlier types of big round baler, and are not to be confused with the small big bales produced by one of the more-recently introduced small big balers.

D. Tomlinson *(Newark Advertiser)*

Ribble Valley garages and filling stations have been warned of a con man who makes his victims pay up to £80 for a bag of flour.

C. Waine *(Lancashire Evening Telegraph)*

Mr Robin Buchanan, chairman of the planning committee, said Bath had a mixed economy. If people used briefcases, it could be that they provided a more convenient way of carrying sandwiches.

G. Stephens *(Bath Evening Chronicle)*

"The butler locks the dining room door and makes a display on the table," continues Lady Harewood. "He does some remarkable things."

S. Jacquet *(Home and Freezer Digest)*

Bangkok will not be flooded this year "unless it is hit by heavy rainfall," City Clerk Thamrong Pattanarat said yesterday.

D. Moreton *(Bangkok Post)*

Vincenzo Mancuso and Calogero Mancuso of Hilberry Avenue, Tuebrook, pleaded guilty at Pontlotyn Magistrates Court to selling an ice cream lolly which was not of the substance demanded in that it contained a portion of human finger.

D. Potter *(Liverpool Daily Post)*

The picket hut built by striking firemen at Grays was so impressive that the men won a competition for the best constructed hut.

W. Cosgrove *(Thurrock Express)*

If you like travelling and prefer working on your own why not try telephone cleaning.

G. Holland Smith *(Islington Gazette)*

Members of Ugley Women's Institute listened to a talk by Miss Gibson, of the Sue Eaton Beauty Clinic.

P. O'Donnell *(Herts & Essex Observer)*

WEATHER. The weather forecast is cancelled today because of the weather. Forecasts are obtained from the airport, and roads there from our office were impassable. Whether we get the weather tomorrow depends on the weather.

A. White *(Saudi Gazette)*

Richmond police reported yesterday that some time between December 1975 and December 1977 something was stolen from Harrod's Depository in Barnes. The loss was reported on Tuesday, but no-one is sure what is missing.

J. Ming *(Barnes, Mortlake and Sheen Herald)*

"I can't see it going down too well with high-powered overseas councillors," he added. "It would have the effect of destroying any goodwill before it was created."

J. Corser *(Woking News & Mail)*

The Board's advisers do not feel that critical appreciation is too difficult for 16 year olds but they consider it is entirely appropriate, in terms of an O-Level examination in drama, to expect candidates both to evaluate their own work and to write critical appraisals of plays and performances seen. Criticisms can be at various levels and candidates who write at the level of, say, the Sunday Times Drama critic would receive full marks.

M. Berry *(Associated Examining Board report)*

Mr Marcus Pearce, prosecuting, said that the accident had been caused by Insp Miller driving round the bend too fast. "The white cat," he said, " was a bit of a red herring if it existed at all."

H. Few *(Harrow Observer)*

Mr John Greace, for Dr Charny, said his client had not been the brains behind the gang. "He was really just a pair of hands."

S. Weston *(Cambridge Evening News)*

Cannabis plants have been found growing in pots in Dawlish Wood. Some of the plants had been badly nibbled by wild animals, which the forest rangers believed were rabbits. "So if anyone sees a rabbit that looks as if it doesn't know if it's coming or going," said the detective, "at least they'll know where it's been."

J. Evans *(Torquay Herald Express)*

This experiment and many others are reported in their fascinating book, with emphasis upon the importance of a diet that builds resistance to such problems as nervousness, irritability, premature ageing and getting more fun out of life.

B. Tovey *(Health Now)*

He pretended his car had broken down and persuaded her to remove her bra for him to mend the car with, it was said.

B. Dawson *(Wolverhampton Express & Star)*

Mr Tim Stone, defending Griffin, said his problems stemmed from drink. He was a registered alcoholic and his thoughts when he jumped into the river was to end it all. Then he remembered he could not swim and called to the policeman for help.

F. Phillips *(Exeter Express & Echo)*

NOTICE TO SHEEP OWNERS. Any sheep found eating the vegetable garden on the Battery property at Clachan will be roasted and served up with potatoes, green peas, mint sauce and redcurrant jelly.

R. McAugthrie *(Campbelltown Courier)*

5 DAY STAY AT HOME HOLIDAYS. Departing weekly—from £26.50.

N. Baines *(Wakefield Express)*

VERY RARE one genuine German steel helmut in first class condition, complete with headphones and microphone, no sensible offers refused.

N. Buchanan *(Blackburn Citizen)*

The Vicar of Otley, Canon D. Kendrick, ate a breakfast of cornflakes in the pulpit of a packed Otley Parish Church in his first Family Harvest Festival at the church to emphasise that many things, including cornflakes, come indirectly from God.

G. Marvill *(Wharfedale and Airedale Observer)*

Mr John Stokes, the Conservative MP for Halesowen and Stourbridge, has broken his shoulder in an accident in Salisbury, Rhodesia. He fell heavily when he took a running jump at a one foot high chain fence outside Government House. Mr Stokes is on a fact finding tour.

J. Gadd *(The County Express)*

Assembly at the City of Portsmouth Girls School began as religious teacher Mr R. Milliken crossed the stage of the hall on a skateboard, colliding with the Minister of Paulsgrove Baptist Church (The Rev. K. W. Rayson). It was a pre-arranged encounter to begin dialogue about building life on Christian foundations.

M. Munro *(The Portsmouth News)*

He was found guilty of knocking down the official and chewing off his ear when he was refused public funds to go to Norway to look for a job. The local court in Nykoebing was told that when the official recovered consciousness after the attack he found his ear on a desk with a note that read: "Your ear."

S. Boothman *(Yorkshire Post)*

Mr Bessell is expected to be in the dock for at least a week. The judge told him to sit down if he wished.

S. Taylor *(Birmingham Evening Mail)*

He said: "I came to Watford to work for my old officer and, one frosty morning, I opened the door of the factory boiler and looked inside. As I walked away there was an explosion in my head and I fell to the ground thinking I had been shot. But it was my glass eye which had exploded because of the sudden change of temperature."

G. Ridgewell *(Watford Evening Echo)*

The only trouble came at nappy changing time. "I am not very experienced at this sort of thing," she said. "But I managed with the help of a traffic warden."

J. S. Butterworth *(Oxford Mail)*

FOREST FIRE DESTROYS TREES

N. Helm *(Hexham Courant)*

"Littleborough has a lot to offer the tourist," Mr Parry said. "But when they come they don't know what it is."

D. Howarth *(Rochdale Observer)*

Wong was visited at his home by all three and after various threats was punched in the face, it was alleged. Eventually he decided to hand over £37, and Chow, who had punched him, gave him 40p change.

P. Sheail *(Enfield Gazette)*

Naming the new village hall at Wilbarston proved more of a problem than the hall committee expected. So they threw the question open to the children of the village, in a "name the hall" competition. Between 30 and 40 youngsters wrote in with their suggestion, which ranged from the topical (Jubilee Hall, Elizabeth II Hall) to the picturesque (Welland View Hall). The committee still couldn't reach a decision so they decided to vote on it. And at the end of the day, Henry Dummer and Katie Bettles, pupils of Wilbarston School, received gift vouchers for their winning name: Wilbarston Village Hall.

H. Hearnshaw *(Harborough Mail)*

Mr. A. R. Cox, counsel for Horvath, said that although the facts were "horrific", the cutting of the body in two pieces was "only because it would not fit into the boot of the Morris Minor," not to avoid detection.

B. Bensley *(Sydney Morning Herald)*

A trip to Blackpool to see the finish of the Milk Race ended unhappily for cyclist Alan Gornall when he had his racing bike stolen. Alan plans to carry on racing without the bike.

S. Neville *(Clitheroe Advertiser)*

Explorer Sir Ranulph Twisleton-Wykeham Fiennes, son of Lady Fiennes, of Lodsworth, who is in a three-man party from the British Transglobe Expedition circumnavigating the world through the two poles, reached the South Pole. Traders in the area reported that Christmas shoppers made a late start.

D. Mason (*Midhurst & Petworth Observer*)

Stir in the tomato puree, tomatoes, green pepper, stock, sugar, bay leaf and dash of nutmeg. Bring everything to the boil and then transfer the stew to a large, deep casserole dish. Cover the cook in the centre of the pre-heated oven for approximately one hour.

L. Brown (*Town Crier*)

Punk rock group The Stranglers made a flying visit to Thame this week when the band's singer, Jean-Jaques Burnell, stopped at Barley's chemist in the High Street to buy some throat lozenges.

C. Overton (*Thame Gazette*)

On larger boats, it's best to stay above deck. Limit eating to dry toast and tea, breathe deeply and keep your eyes off the waves. Speak softly and carry a big plastic bag.

D. Huegel (*Allentown Chronicle*)

FRIDAY CLUB: As its name implies, the club meets on Thursdays at the Robert Bakewell School, with table tennis, darts, discos and soccer.

T. Barnsley (*Loughborough Echo*)

INFORMATION WANTED. Dr Ingram F. Anderson is interested to hear from anyone who knows of any silent films featuring Caruso singing.

N. Posner (*Gramophone*)

The Belgian Consul in Miami, Gui Govaert, said Dussart's case is easy to resolve. "If he can present himself to me and establish he is who he is, I can sign and verify that he is he. Then we can send the certificate to Brussels and find out very quickly whether he is dead or alive."

J. Sutherland (*Miami News*)

TEACHING POSTS IN GREECE. Duties: to teach English as a foreign language at all levels, from beginners to advanced. Qualifications: Candidates should be native speakers, have a degree either in English (Language and/or Literature) or Linguistics, or something.

J. Kilner (*Times Educational Supplement*)

A quick bit of detecting established that the crocodile was one of two, both named George, and that it came from the nearby Country Club.

J. Bullett *(Salisbury Herald)*

AIR BVI REQUIRES STEWARDESSES for immediate employment. Minimum age 17 years. Must be in good health and be able to swim.

S. Dick-Read *(British Virgin Islands Sun)*

Breathing is a natural thing, the first reflex action at birth, and the habit which lasts a lifetime.

R. Hankinson *(Cranleigh Times)*

Defending solicitor Mr Richard Snow suggested that Brother Finbarr, a teacher, was mistaken in identifying his client as he had spoken to him through a row of runner beans.

M. Rendall *(Western Gazette)*

Mr Ted Bean, Miss Sarah Harny and Mr Tony Evans, none of whom has any parachuting experience, take to the air on Sunday afternoon. The only training they will have is a few hours practice the day after the jump.

P. Wyatt *(Banbury Guardian)*

Lighting-up time doesn't mean a lot to people living near 79 Kingsway, Rochdale—where a lamp has been positioned so its rays are shrouded by the leaves of a tree. And Mr Edward Goodwin says that when he complained about the lamp, he was told: "Don't worry. You'll be all right in Autumn. The leaves will fall off."

D. Howarth *(Rochdale Observer)*

For decorating the tops of salads with political slogans and symbols, a Hampshire College student lost his job. The firing was for refusing to obey orders to stop doing such things as writing "No Nukes" on the tops of salads with carrot sticks and making hammer and sickle designs in wax on the cottage cheese.

C. Pike *(Boston Globe)*

Police are questioning participants at a group therapy session in Dreux, France, in which a man died when four people walked on him to stamp out his complexes.   M. Robinson *(Yorkshire Post)*

It was a training workshop on how to conduct training workshops. It begs the questions of where the people conducting the training workshop got their training to conduct a workshop to train people to conduct a workshop.

D. Benton *(Lebanon Valley News)*

28

A New Zealand trapper lost in bush-covered mountains for three weeks survived by eating raw rats—which he made more palatable by pretending they were baked beans.

W. Towne *(Lancashire Evening Post)*

A Malvern motorist who drove his car on the wrong side of the road and ran off when police caught up with him, refused a breath test on the grounds that he was a pedestrian, the town's magistrates heard.

J. Mitchell *(The Malvern Gazette and Ledbury Reporter)*

Daniels told the court that he and Livings were "a bit hungry" and so they thought they would take a couple of apples. Fining each man a total of £50, Mr T W Passey, presiding, told them they must have been hungry to steal half-a-hundredweight of apples.

R. Andrews *(The Ross Gazette)*

Under the scheme, each 800-soldier-strong Battle Group spends one month being welded together to become one of the Army's basic mechanised fighting teams.

L. Walsh *(Golbourne Report and Star)*

In a report to a local Chamber of Commerce and Industry, Mr Robert Rumbold, area superintendent of the bus company, says: "Service reliability slipped up somewhat during this holiday period. This was mainly due to considerable absenteeism during the feast of Ramadan."

D. Dell *(Beds and Bucks Observer)*

The key witness said that he had gone to school for only one day but had learned to speak English in the bars. He said that was in 1966, and he had been born in 1956. He said he was then twenty years old. Asked why there was a discrepancy, Wachira Ndirangu said that although he had learnt to speak English in bars, he had not had the opportunity to learn Mathematics.

R. Wilding *(Nairobi Standard)*

A mushroom with a diameter of 10 inches was picked this week by Mr James Johnson, Delhi Road, Eastriggs in the Ministry of Defence depot at Eastriggs where he works. A fortnight ago he picked another giant mushroom eight inches in diameter.

M. Kirk *(Cumberland News)*

Rubber was the theme of a talk by Mrs. B. Percy to Wingrave Methodist women's meeting. She brought along various items, linking them with aspects of the Christian way of life.

M. Buchanan *(Beds and Bucks Observer)*

Batsmen playing for St. Anne's second team against Fleetwood in the Northern League yesterday found runs frustratingly hard to come by. Then after more than two hours' play the reason dawned on them— Fleetwood had 12 men on the field. The mistake came to light when there were not enough meals to go round at the interval.

H. Knight *(Lancashire Evening Telegraph)*

Uruguay has just experienced what must rank as the strangest transfer of all time. The "World Soccer" magazine reports that one, Daniel Allende, has moved from second-division club Central Espanol to the first-division side Rentistas—for 550 beef steaks with the payment being made at 25 steaks a week.

G. Scandrett *(Glasgow Herald)*

"The people of Marston Green are being raped and most of them are lying back and thinking of aeroplanes," he said.

M. Hill *(Solihull News)*

Asked why the books show £5,000 owed in arrears, deputy housing manager Wilf Pickett told the housing committee that nearly half the figure was accountable to former tenants. "These are people who have died without giving us notice," he explained.

F. Donovan *(St. Albans Review and Express)*

"I was watching the terrace riots in Italy last week and thought how pleasant it was that dominoes does not have this sort of trouble," said Mr Stock. "Now I'm not so sure."

T. Arthur *(Western Telegraph)*

This led to the publication by Academic Press in 1961 of the world's first book on organoboron chemistry, which proved so popular that it was translated into Russian.

R. Cross *(Chemistry in Britain)*

Horsham Cricket Club skipper Richard Marshall called for the wearing of helmets at the club's annual dinner in the clubhouse on Friday. "If ever there is a case for club batsmen wearing helmets it must be now," he said.

J. Urwin *(West Sussex Country Times)*

The sudden fierce gust of wind took all who were at the ceremony completely by surprise. Hats were blown off and copies of the Vicar's speech and other rubbish were scattered over the site.

J. Eastwood *(Ninfield and Hooe Parish News)*

All my life I wanted to be a barrow boy
A barrow boy I've always wanted to be.

An Aviemore man who claimed his spectacles had been broken when he was the victim of a mugging attack stole a magnifying glass so that he could look for a job, Inverness Sheriff Court heard yesterday.

M. Chisholm *(Aberdeen Press and Journal)*

Bristol's 18th Century Blaise Castle Folly is to be partly demolished and left as a conserved ruin if the city council agrees.

R. Ford *(Western Daily Press)*

Mrs Hilda Isherwood has lost count of the number of times she has seen the dawn coming up over her ironing board.

C. Waine *(Lancashire Evening Telegraph)*

When the news of Sir John's death was announced at a dance being held in Tesco County Club the stunned audience held a minute's silence before bursting into a chorus of "I Always Wanted to be a Barrow Boy."

P. Lane *(Lea Valley Mercury)*

The concert, which was relayed "live" on BBC Radio Three and Four, opened promisingly with Svendsen's "Carnival in Paris." In this, we were able to catch much of the authentic atmosphere of the Scandinavian fjords.

M. Taylor *(Lancashire Evening Post)*

A Langley man became so "frustrated" at seeing a neighbour's cat scratching the roof of his £3,000 car that he got an air rifle and shot at it. When asked by an RSPCA Inspector why he did not throw a bucket of water over the cat instead, he said: "I didn't want to get the car wet." N. Ashman *(Windsor, Slough and Eton Express)*

"When I was living in a house with an upstairs toilet, I applied for a grant to construct a downstairs toilet and the social work department wrote back to say despite my wheelchair, I didn't qualify but would I like a knitting machine instead?"

J. Audis *(Edinburgh Evening News)*

There must, for instance, be something very strange in a man who, if left alone in a room with a teacosy, doesn't try it on.

T. McCormick *(Glasgow Evening Times)*

Mrs Abkar read some of her own poems and Mrs Sylvia D'Alcorn won a prize for her candle decorated in blue and silver. Mrs M. Cannon was also a prize winner, she won a jar of Bovril in the tombola.

J. Lewis *(Richmond and Twickenham Times)*

Police officers were called to the Harbour, and in spite of language difficulties, the problem was soon resolved with the help of a police alsatian.

K. Grant *(Jersey Evening Post)*

Colour TV, 22in only green colour working, £60.

D. Campbell *(Surrey Mirror)*

Police yesterday warned people at Bradford to be wary of bogus frogs.

J. Cochrane *(Yorkshire Post)*

"Deaths are on the decline and Portchester Crematorium has had its worst year since 1972–73," its Superintendent, Mr Edward Appleton, told Portchester Crematorium Joint Committee meeting at Portsmouth Guildhall.

L. Brice *(Portsmouth News)*

A trade union has reported that a request to expunge the word "shirty" from the Oxford English dictionary has been turned down. *The Garment Worker* says the managing director of Tern Shirts told the dictionary editors that the connotations of bad temper contained in the word were damaging to the shirt manufacturing industry.

G. Ridgewell *(Luton Evening Post)*

What's the best way to bury a supply of gold or silver coins, or perhaps an extra rifle and ammunition? *Personal Finance* suggests using PVC plastic pipe, which has largely replaced copper in plumbing applications. It comes in many diameters, from 1-inch to 12-inches. Smaller diameters can be found in hardware stores, the larger sizes at plumbing or irrigation supply houses.

P. Dyball *(American Personal Finance)*

As a future business person, I take personal exception to the statement that business people as a group are cultural philistines. The reason why some of us have not yet got around to reading Anna Karenina may simply be because we don't like Dickens.

E. Gow *(Toronto Globe and Mail)*

The best Mass, according to one woman, is at Earlwood. "Where we used to go, Mass took an hour," she said, "so we shopped around and switched to Earlwood. It's a lovely Mass there, and it's over in 35 minutes."

J. Clarke *(Sydney Sun-Herald)*

A woman's relationship with her partner had "deepened and matured" since she stuck a kitchen knife in his chest.

D. Wilby *(Pontefract and Castleford Express)*

The list of ingredients for creamy rice (Epicure 8/5) omitted rice. The recipe requires ½ cup of uncooked rice.

J. Wadsley *(Melbourne Age)*

George, 58, began playing the piano in a South London pub when 16 and worked his way up to playing trumpet solos on his accordian in the Willy Lark band.

A. Pryor *(Kent Messenger)*

Malvern water is not worth thinking about but the egg sandwiches served at Worcester Railway Station buffet are of high nutritional value.

S. Bishop *(Hereford Evening News)*

The thieves broke in in broad daylight on Bank Holiday Monday afternoon, eating through a louvre window.

J. Howse *(Bournemouth Evening Echo)*

Perth and Kinross District Council yesterday dropped a plan to celebrate the Government's new May Day holiday on January 2.

J. Campbell *(The Scotsman)*

If you have a sack that is full of holes don't throw it away, empty them out into a clean box and store in the dry; they may be useful when you start bulb planting.

H. Burkinshaw *(Horticultural Corporation's Garden Topics)*

Ways of trying to make sure people in Keyworth know the date of the annual parish meeting are being tried by the parish council. They are to have posters printed and displayed in several places in the village.

M. Fitzgerald *(Nottingham Evening Post)*

The Egyptian Defence Minister, Lt. Gen. Ahmed Badawi, a hero of Arab wars against Israel and 13 other military commanders, died yesterday when their helicopter hit a lamp-post and crashed at a desert oasis.

D. Barrett *(Yorkshire Post)*

WANTED. Secondhand bagpipes, any make other than Pakistani.
J. Burns (*Rolls-Royce News*)

Chairman had to call: "I think we'd better all sit down and see how we stand."
R. Edwards (*East Anglian Magazine*)

HE CATHEDRAL PRIVATE CLINIC. Hair transplants and sectomy. Congratulations to the Prince of Wales and Lady Diana.
T. Atkinson (*South Wales Echo*)

"I find it astonishing that those residents who are quick to come along to collect free bus travel tokens cannot show their faces for the annual meeting. It would only take a minute for them to get into their cars and drive to the public car park across the way."
M. Chase (*West Sussex County Times*)

FOR SALE. Genuine Russian Balilika, as new, no music, £15. Exchange Wall Gas Heater, no flue.
J. Maling (*King's Lynn News & Advertiser*)

Mr Goodman gave an interesting talk, accompanied with film, on the subject, Wildlife in Care. A vote of thanks was given by Mrs Delia Fox.
H. Hindley (*Hastings & St Leonards Observer*)

Archer said to WPC Caroline Stephenson: "If you arrest me I'll mark your face for life." She then kicked the officer in the leg, added Insp. Peters.
G. Heppell (*Yorkshire Evening Press*)

If the reader signing himself "Homeless" will let us know his full name and address—not for publication—we will be pleased to give space to his letter.
J. Judge (*Glasgow Evening Leader*)

A schoolboy's head had become stuck in a vase. His mother was shing him off to hospital. Presumably in order to avoid attracting tention, she had placed her son's school cap on top of the vase."
B. Lacey (*Western Daily Press*)

Power demand went up by 1,200 MW when BBC screened the final of the Miss World Contest. The biggest increase in demand was during the cabaret act by Frank Ifield when people switched kettles on.

B. G. Dobbs *(Power News)*

The new bus shelters in Pittenweem have been erected on the wrong side of the bus stops. The Town Council is to rectify the matter by moving the bus stops to the other end of the bus shelters.

A. P. Fyffe *(Dundee Courier & Advertiser)*

Paper sacks can be obtained at the Cardross Mill filling station, Rhu public convenience, Arrochar public convenience, Garelochhead Health Centre and from the street sweeper in Rosneath.

G. M. Bucknall *(Helensburgh Advertiser)*

Fourteen-year-old Christopher Swallow, younger son of Mr and Mrs Alfred H. Swallow, is a boy whom his grandmother would be proud of. For she was one of the original Tiller Girls and her grandson seems to be following in her footsteps.

D. Roberts *(Chester Chronicle)*

We understand these jobs can be boring and we do all we can. We play music while you work and we show factory safety films and cartoons in break times. There is a chiropodist who calls.

R. P. & C. Hartley *(Birmingham Post)*

They heard Mr Heffron trace the changing role of the solicitor since the 16th century when his firm was started. The competition for a dressed wooden spoon was won by Mrs Johnson.

C. M. Pozzi *(Welwyn Times)*

He said that the Post Office unions were specially active in helping Post Office workers in Bangladesh and in the African countries, adding that the gift of three ballpoint pens could enable three new union branches to start in Bangladesh.

A. Carr *(Norfolk News)*

The best-dressed owner and dog prize
went to Mrs. Gladys Martin of Ton-
bridge, and her spaniel, as Maid Marion
and Robin Hood. Best-dressed owner
was a Hastings member, disguised as a
bone.
   T. J. Lunn *(Kent & Sussex Courier)*

The report follows recent "sightings" of a lion in Nottinghamshire, one of which turned out to be a paper bag.

T. Hopkins *(Luton Evening Post)*

Whenever the Vicar of Leeds, Canon Graham Foley, attends luncheons and dinners at the Queen's Hotel his place setting is the only one without a bread roll.

J. Harvey *(Yorkshire Post)*

A woman was rushed to a hospital's intensive care unit last night after she collapsed following a decision to build a cattery next to her home.

A. Laidlaw (*Northern Echo*)

Scouts have cancelled their planned old folks' Christmas party after being blamed for blocking drains with sandwiches.

A. Rootes (*Kent Messenger*)

A sheriff ordered a social inquiry report on a dog yesterday after hearing it had taken part in an attempted robbery.

J. G. Williamson (*Glasgow Herald*)

An amateur gardener whose seed potatoes were stolen six months ago wrote to his local newspaper giving the thief hints on how to grow them. Mr Harry Dorling, of Weston Ridge, Otley, has now received a parcel of potatoes from the thief—"Mr X"—through the post, with hints on how to cook them.

M. H. Bowling *(Yorkshire Post)*

A 19-year-old Plumley man who had been celebrating in Northwich did not realise he had stolen a bicycle until he fell off it, Northwich magistrates were told last week.   C. Blackman *(Northwich Guardian)*

P.C. Gordon Wilkinson said that Catchum was wearing a maxi-coat, flowered hot pants, knee-length boots, pink glasses, make-up and carrying a handbag. He said he had gone into the toilet for natural reasons.

C. B. Davies *(Exeter Express & Echo)*

A holly tree in Cookham is to be painted white because locals have complained that they have been scratched by its prickly branches while walking past it at night.

M. Flemins *(The Sunday Press)*

Horses which bit and gouged two orange-coloured cars may have thought they were giant carrots, it was suggested today.

D. Baker *(Bristol Evening Post)*

Double yellow lines which were up to half an inch thick because of over-painting were causing cyclists to wobble off their bikes, Cheshire Police Committee were told yesterday.

E. Brown *(Liverpool Daily Post)*

All sorts of household "waste" can be re-used if we stop to think. Toilet rolls, for instance, can be painted with black lacquer to make napkin rings.

B. R. Nunn *(Woman's Journal)*

The couple were married at Kensington Register Office. Virginia, who is 26, wore a short, bright yellow, woollen shirt-waister. Lord Ashcombe, who is 48 and head of Cubitts, the building firm, wore a heavy overcoat.

J. Whitfield *(Dorking Advertiser)*

In a statement, Bolderstone said he took the road sign because he thought it would look nice with the wallpaper in his home. Mr. G. G. Thomas, chairman, told Bolderstone it was a public nuisance when people took road signs.

S. R. Wilson *(Westmorland Gazette)*

Oristano, Sardinia.—Belgian cyclist Eddy Merckx captured the Tour of Sardinia today, winning three million lire ($4,500) and a silver medal from Pope Paul VI, a cycling enthusiast.

P. Hopkinson *(International Herald Tribune)*

Four people wearing size ten shoes have twice as much area in contact with the ground as the average family saloon car, says the monthly accident bulletin issued by Warwickshire police.

M. Carter *(Leamington Spa Courier)*

Liquorice allsorts played an important part in the February meeting of Cholesbury-cum-St. Leonard's W.I. Mrs. Betty Wilson exhibited a birthday card decorated with a floral design in dried foliage and English allsorts and the lecture, given by Mrs. Jenny Martin, whose home town is Maastricht, was on Dutch liquorice allsorts.

W. Patterson *(Bucks Examiner)*

A housewife, who asked not to be named because she was afraid of possible reprisals, has complained that one salesman, acting on behalf of a well-known soft drinks firm, rattled his false teeth at her when she showed reluctance to buy and she was so intimidated that she immediately rang her neighbours to warn them.

A. Fitton *(Southport Visiter)*

Two tabby cats, Quicksilver and Quince, have given £2 each towards the Lincoln Cathedral Preservation Fund. They belong to Miss Beatrice Hill, of Cumbria, and have their own bank account with their names printed on the cheques, which Miss Hill countersigns.

P. Vuckovic *(Doncaster Evening Post)*

Three police cars and an ambulance rushed to a flat in Fort Pitt Street, Chatham, after home-help Mrs. Patricia Marshall reported seeing a body in the bath. But she was mistaken. What she had seen, when she had peeped through the letter-box after failing to get an answer, was a woman's wig on a hat-stand.

N. L. Starkey *(Chatham Standard)*

A lady of many hobbies, she makes woollen rabbits and, on the political front, she recently read a book by Enoch Powell.

S. Coltman *(Bournemouth Echo)*

Said Mr Metcalfe: "This will be a very exacting type of expedition and one which will sort out the wheat from the chaff. It is not everybody's cup of tea. It teaches them to stand on their feet in an age when everything is handed to them on a plate."

P. J. Hare *(Glasgow Evening Times)*

A barrister told Bradford magistrates yesterday that if a firm's output of cheese slices were placed end to end it would be necessary to walk 4,412 miles before finding a mouldy one.

M. J. Robinson *(Yorkshire Post)*

Monkeys have gone on strike on a coconut plantation near Kuantan, Malaysia.

J. M. Shaw *(Voice of Uganda)*

A Devon man has invented wellington boots which light up when there is dangerous gas about.
                    C. B. Davies *(Exeter Express & Echo)*

Farmers on Humberside have been warned to watch out for fake courting couples who cuddle in cars while their accomplices steal sheep, lambs, or potatoes.
                    E. G. Breeze *(Yorkshire Post)*

When police found 17-year-old Michael Siddall outside a town-centre shop in the early hours of the morning he told them he was looking for a pound which he had lost. At first he denied having anything to do with a knife which was stuck in the door. However he then admitted that he had bought the knife to peel potatoes with at the same time that he had bought a tea strainer.

P. Hollindale (*The Derbyshire Times*)

A Santa Claus parachuting to open a Christmas fair at Liversedge, near Bradford, on Saturday was blown off course and landed a mile-and-a-half away at Hartshead.

R. O. Kohner *(Yorkshire Post)*

Palmers Green—or more precisely the roof of 75 Derwent Road—is a landmark in the history of aviation. It is very probably the first roof in London to have stopped a crashing aircraft.

R. Williamson (*Palmers Green and Southgate Gazette*)

Anger is growing among shopkeepers in a Bedfordshire village over a new market which has been set up under a flag showing a pregnant spook.

T. Hopkins (*Luton Evening Post*)

Browned off, a sugar boiler and lettering artist from Cleveleys, relieved his feelings by inserting a five letter rude word in more than a thousand sticks of Torquay rock.

W. Watkinson (*Lancashire Life*)

Stan, an airedale terrier who wore contact lenses, has been run over by a car in Bilbao.

S. Todd *(Evening Standard)*

Most of us parents know that, in order to keep down the price of school lunches, meat in some dishes is being partly or wholly replaced by protein made from soya beans. But what about the Cambridgeshire school which is offering its pupils fried cod-pieces?

E. G. Breeze *(Public Service)*

Richmond-upon-Thames amenities committee has decided against putting a fence round Kneller Gardens, Twickenham, to prevent vandalism because they felt the fence would be damaged by vandals.

J. Scott *(Richmond & Twickenham Times)*

For his ten years as the union branch secretary, a task described as "thankless" by both himself and his colleagues, a wall clock was given to him as a small compensation, also a large sack full of elastic bands.

A. Wood *(Stratford Herald)*

Most of the unusually high number of schizophrenic breakdown patients in the Republic of Ireland are single, a health research report says today.

D. M. Copp *(Birmingham Mail)*

A man walking in the street in Luneville, France, was shot in the shoulder by a dog firing from a hotel window, police said today.

C. M. Hallam (*Bath & West Evening Chronicle*)

A change of name to Data Products (Dublin) Memories Ltd has been announced by what was formerly Data Products/Core Memories Ltd. The change has been carried out to clear up an ambiguous situation where although Core Memories Ltd. was established in Dublin eight years ago as a subsidiary of Data Products Corp, it had become known in Europe as Data Products/Core Memories Ltd.

H. J. Fisher (*Computer Weekly*)

"Queer sticks" were the subject of a talk at the monthly meeting of the Worsley Afternoon Townswomen's Guild. Presenting the illustrated talk was Mr Greenup who showed a varied collection of sticks and gave anecdotes of friends and acquaintances of whom they remind him.

G. S. Schajer *(Swinton & Pendlebury Journal)*

An invoice for £11.83 issued by North East Fife District Council to an Anstruther woman for the hire of Cellardyke Town Hall, for a going-away party, has been written off. All reminders have been returned marked "gone away".

D. Purdie *(Fife Herald News)*

PC Scales decided to search Wellington who pulled out a tobacco tin and held it behind his back. Wellington then pushed PC Scales in the chest and when PC Mills came to his assistance Wellington turned on him and in the violent struggle butted him in the face and kicked him in the groin. Wellington was carried into a police van and was abusive at the police station but later apologised for his behaviour. The tobacco tin was found to contain cigarette papers and shreds of tobacco.

R. Coode *(Edmonton Weekly Herald)*

He said he had been to settle an old score with someone living there, but had not been able to do so. Goodman explained that another reason for carrying the knife, apart from self-defence, had been to free his foot when the swivel joint on the artificial leg became jammed in wet weather.

N. Pattison *(Gloucestershire Echo)*

Watching sport on television brings to mind the image of a troup of orang-outangs, trained as fairground barkers and then asked to explain Einstein's theory of relativity in a live relay from the moon.

T. Hopkins (*Luton Evening Post*)

Two crash helmets have been stolen from a garage at Shelley Road, Bath and a number of piglets stolen from a farm at Wellow.

S. Wayne (*Bath and West Evening Chronicle*)

Magistrates in Cumbria agreed to call the defendant Mr X. This was merely because nobody knew how to pronounce the man's name. Mr Eric Arnison, the acting clerk, suggested the alternative after running into trouble with the name—Kamarudin Bin Xhmxo.

A. I. Riach *(Yorkshire Post)*

They bought the 30-year-old boat in Plymouth from three Australians, of whom the skipper, John Dolman, was in fact a prospective crew member. However, he has now decided to go overland to Australia in a motor boat.

P. M. Cutter (*Western Evening News*)

Everything at the Mill Hotel, Sunbury has run smoothly since a mummified cat was replaced beneath the floor.

M. Boyle *(Ipswich Evening Star)*

While he was drunk, a Shrewsbury man tried to climb a ladder he was carrying.

R. Jamieson *(Shrewsbury Chronicle)*

Eighty-four per cent of the population in much of South-East London live within five minutes walk of a bus-stop. This is one conclusion of a joint GLC-London Transport study.

C. Maddock *(Kentish Times)*

When the Information Centre in Greenock opened today to give away the first of thousands of trees there was a queue of seven dogs. One was an old English sheepdog.

C. Elliott *(Greenock Telegraph)*

An Oxford man hit his wife's lover over the head with a hammer after inviting him to his house to talk things over, Oxford Crown Court heard yesterday.

J. C. Wood *(Oxford Mail)*

Mr. Thomas Proudfoot, aged 66, reached out for a blackberry yesterday and spent nearly six hours trapped in a bramble bush near the North Riding village of Wilton.

W. Molyneaux *(Birmingham Post)*

Sales of oranges are booming in Singapore after an English housewife declared that rubbing them into her husband's hair was a good cure for baldness.

F. Martell *(Bradford Telegraph & Argus)*

Ashford police were told last Thursday that a lorry was shedding marmalade along Ashford Road at Bethersden. They said that no traffic jam was caused.

P. Brook *(Kentish Express)*

A survey showing that one in five of Birmingham's policemen is married to a nurse has led to a joint recruiting week-end. The organisers hope to recruit policemen and nurses.

M. Harper *(Southern Evening Echo)*

Housewife Diane Cove thought she had found a piece of fish skin in a bottle of milk. But when it was examined by a public health inspector it was found to be a piece of cardboard saying "No milk today, thank-you."

T. Hopkins *(Luton Evening Post)*

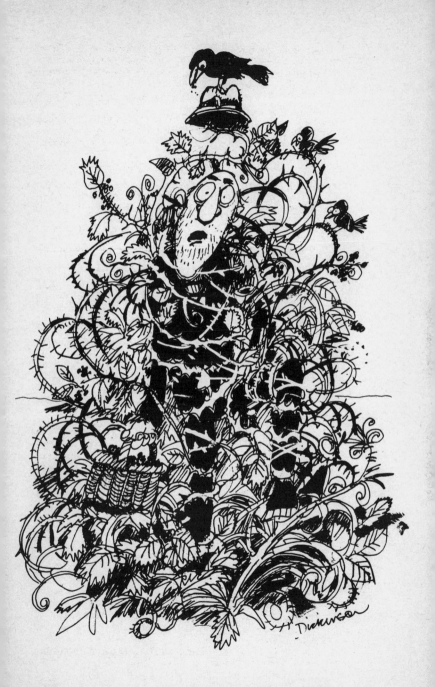

Glasgow District Council has already received reports of dampness from other housing schemes—and at one stage officials claimed that condensation in the Hutchesontown flats was due to "tenant's heavy breathing".

W. King *(Glasgow Evening Times)*

Instant coffee will give you more value if you slightly reduce the amount on the spoon and adjust the amount of milk.

V. Frankl *(Middlesbrough Evening Gazette)*

A combination of comradeship and crisps played its part in strengthening Anglo-Russian relations when a party of eight wrestlers from Russia visited the Great Harwood factory of XL Crisps on Thursday morning.

A. English *(Accrington Observer)*

Police are hunting a middle-aged couple who kidnapped a tortoise. Topsy was sunning herself on the front lawn of Mr and Mrs Derham's home in Thatcham, Berks, when a car stopped and a woman got out. She bundled Topsy into the car and they sped off.

J. Cochrane (*Yorkshire Post*)

Elton John, the superstar who can afford to pay £8,000 for a pair of platinum-studded spectacles, will not be at Armley on Friday.

W. Rothschild *(Bradford Telegraph & Argus)*

A doctor who had too much to drink blamed a patient's chest spasms on the fact that he was childless, a disciplinary committee was told yesterday. But while it was true the man had no children, it was also true he had been married only two weeks, said Mr. Paul Honigmann, for the General Medical Council.

E. Leslie *(Dundee Courier & Advertiser)*

The difference between a menhir and a menhaden is that a menhir is a single tall upright stone set up as a monument and a menhaden is a kind of large herring found on the East Coast of the United States yielding oil and used as manure.

J. Harvey *(Nottingham Evening Post)*

Life in a glue factory was described by Robert Baggs when members of Richmond branch of the International Friendship League chatted about their jobs on Monday evening.

J. Scott *(Putney & Roehampton Herald)*

Police are looking for a missing estate of 119 houses, complete with roads, lamp standards and trees.

J. Cochrane *(Yorkshire Post)*

Ellen Donna Cooperman sought to push women's liberation to new lengths, but failed, in New York. A judge turned down her request to change her name to Ellen Donna Cooperperson. He said she was being silly.

J. Akroyd *(Halifax Evening Courier)*

Great Dane enthusiasts are worried about the image of the breed. One said : "It would be tragic if Great Danes became associated with pornography in the mind of the public."

T. Hopkins *(Luton Evening Post)*

Rockfist was born in the mind of Mr. Frank Pepper and he first appeared in the pages of The Champion, a boys' comic, in October 1938. He finally left the scene some 1,000 chapters and five million words later on May 6, 1961. And considering thát Leo Tolstoy used 700,000 words in "War and Peace" that must put Rockfist among the all-time greats of fiction.

R. H. Davis *(Liverton Gazette)*

Castle Rising's gamekeeper, Mr H. Felstead, had a moth in his ear on Monday. He had just gone to bed when the moth disrupted his sleep by entering the inside of his ear and fluttering about. His wife, Elizabeth, poured olive oil into the ear, which killed the moth. Next day, Mr Felstead went to Lynn General Hospital to have the moth removed. Doctors were surprised at its size, it was one of the very large type moths. Mr Felstead now has the moth in a bottle.

L. Hersch *(Lynn News & Advertiser)*

Ambulancemen driving down Elms Vale Road, Dover, yesterday swung into action when they saw a man lying on his garden path with his legs out onto the pavement. One of the ambulancemen ran over to him with re-suscitation equipment, while his colleague grabbed a stretcher. But they found the man was just trying to turn the water stopcock off.

E. Hadaway *(East Kent Mercury)*

Claims that Surrey Heath dustmen have been collecting refuse in their own cars, run on the council's petrol, have been dismissed as rubbish.

J. Millett *(Woking News & Mail)*

Nearly 600 people were bashed and robbed during a Stevie Wonder outdoor concert in Washington to celebrate Human Kindness Day.

W. Hardy *(Sydney Daily Telegraph)*

When a 27-year-old Bible student moved into a flat at Brixton he had a vision from God that the rent he was paying was too high, the landlords claimed.

C. Worsley *(South London Press)*

Lincolnshire police now wear instantly detachable clip-on ties instead of the conventional knotted ones. A spokesman said: "Some policemen raised the point that on a number of occasions men seized their ties and swung on them."

T. J. Lawson *(Portsmouth News)*

Top Tips. When gathering washing in from the line, leave a pillow-case until the last, using it to pop all the smaller things in. This saves time and lost socks, I find.

M. M. Willoughby *(Exmouth Weekly Times)*

And at 244 Calais Road, Mrs Monica Evans told police she was working at her kitchen sink when she saw lightning travel up her legs, through her body and out through her stomach. She was said to be suffering from "slight shock". However, there could be more stormy weather ahead.

P. J. Thorp *(Burton Daily Mail)*

A man entered his ex-wife's house, set light to her coat and spectacles and put some of her jewellery into a full pot of jam, Rochdale magistrates heard on Monday.

P. C. Fitton *(Rochdale Observer)*

Because of the possible danger and nuisance caused in school playgrounds by stray dogs, head teachers in various Barnsley area schools may be issued with lassoes.

D. Brice *(Barnsley Chronicle)*

When Mr Gerry Smith, an income tax inspector, walked on to a building site dressed as a navvy, seven men dropped their tools, jumped over a fence and haven't been seen since.

B. A. Lacey *(Hereford Times)*

The Rector writes: "When Jesus said to the Disciples, after the feeding of the 5,000, 'Gather up the fragments that remain' he may not have been thinking primarily about litter—there would have been no wrappings in that case."

H. Godfrey (*The Visitor*)

He was called one day to a house on the Riddings estate where a woman had reported a rat tangled up in her washer. She told Maurice that she first decided to call the fire brigade, then she realised her husband was a fireman. But he was upstairs and would not come down.

J. A. Taylor *(Scunthorpe Star)*

When a letter from Cumbria County Council was read out asking the council's advice about having a "kissing gate" at Well Lane/Pigeon Well Lane, Lonning, Mr Brian Ashmore said: "There's enough kissing goes on down there without providing a gate for it."

W. Ewart *(West Cumberland Times and Star)*

For the company, Mr. R. Southcombe submitted that at the moment of sale at the company's Ditchling Road shop there was no proof that the staple was in the cake. It was possible it got into the cake by a "freak process" while Mr. Bronwick's wife was taking it home.

A. Russell-Taylor *(Brighton Evening Argus)*

"We arrived to find a man who appeared to be foaming round the mouth," said P.C. Victor Harrison. "Later it was ascertained that he had been eating yoghurt," he added.

L. Colin *(Barnet Press)*

Any flies buzzing around Kensington Palace in future could be in for a big shock, for Princess Margaret yesterday found a machine that attracts flies and kills them with a 4,500-volt shock. She told the man who demonstrated it to her at a Manchester exhibition that she "needed" one and took a pamphlet home with her.

M. J. Robinson *(Yorkshire Post)*

At the end of Hamilton Rotary Club's recent "International Night", attended by a number of students from various parts of the world the Rev Andrew M. Douglas made an impassioned plea for better understanding among nations and people. At the club's next meeting the speaker will be talking on "gun manufacturing".

K. Forrest *(Hamilton Advertiser)*

He works on the principle that the customer is always right. "I once had to kick someone out because he insisted on steak and a bottle of wine at four in the morning. But Horlicks at five is perfectly reasonable because we are able to do that," he said.

C. B. Keylock *(Western Daily Press)*

Exeter, Devon, couple Raymond and Sandra Prin are quitting their home because of a ghost which, they say, tripped up their baby son and said sorry.

P. Clarke *(Basildon Evening Echo)*

LOST: Parrot, green, Lansdown area. Probably walking.

S. Wayne *(Bath & Wilts Evening Chronicle)*

Referring to the fact that the early church was sent to preach the gospel to the ends of the earth, he said the ends of the earth included Hitchen.

R. Potter *(North Herts Gazette)*

Edwina MacKenzie, almost 91, credits her long life to having decided to get off the Titanic after it hit an iceberg 63 years ago.

A. Lawrie *(Globe and Mail, Toronto)*

A mystery man surprised customers and assistants at the Rosary newsagents, Halfway, Walton, by walking through the front window without stopping.

J. Scott *(Surrey Herald)*

A Channel tunnel will cut flying time to Paris from Heathrow by almost an hour, it was revealed last week.

C. Willis *(Journal of Commerce)*

When teacher Mike Hedley was given a hot cross bun he nailed it to a beam and put his name beside it instead of eating it.

T. Hopkins *(Luton Evening Post)*

A boy who preferred going to sea to going to school was told by a judge yesterday to keep out of trouble and be sure to keep within the 200 mile limit.

J. Harvey *(Yorkshire Post)*

Dentists are losing trade to Bostik No. 1 clear adhesive it seems. More and more people are using it to repair their false teeth.

J. Karas *(Croydon Advertiser)*